SAFETY

DURING EMERGENCIES

by Lucia Raatma

THE CHILD'S WORLD®

C H A N H A S S E N ,   M I N N E S O T A

The Child's World

Published in the United States of America by the Child's World®
P.O. Box 326, Chanhassen, MN 55317-0326
800-599-READ
www.childsworld.com

Subject Consultant:
David Zielinski,
Manager of Chapter
Developed Programs,
American Red Cross
of Chicago, Chicago,
Illinois

Photo Credits: Cover: Corbis; Corbis: 9 (Joseph Sohm; ChromoSohm Inc.), 21 (Owaki-Kulla), 22 (Richard Hutchings), 23 (Bob Rowan; Progressive Image); Corbis/Picture Quest: 10 right, 12; David Young-Wolff/PhotoEdit: 17; Getty Images/Photodisc: 8, 17 right (Ryan McVay), 18; Photodisc/Punchstock: 5 (Eyewire), 15 right, 20, 25 right; Picture Quest: 6 (Keith Brofsky/Photodisc), 7 (Digital Vision), 11 (Radlund & Associates/Brand X Pictures), 25 (Creatas), 26 (Ryan McVay/Photodisc); Punchstock: 10 (Image Source), 13 (Banana Stock), 19 (Corbis); Stockbyte/Punchstock: 15, 24.

The Child's World®: Mary Berendes, Publishing Director

Editorial Directions, Inc.:E. Russell Primm, Editorial Director; Elizabeth K. Martin and Katie Marsico, Line Editors; Olivia Nellums, Editorial Assistant; Susan Hindman, Copy Editor; Susan Ashley, Proofreader; Peter Garnham, Fact Checker; Tim Griffin/IndexServ, Indexer; Elizabeth K. Martin and Matthew Messbarger, Photo Researchers and Selectors

Library of Congress Cataloging-in-Publication Data
Raatma, Lucia.
  Safety during emergencies / by Lucia Raatma.
      p. cm. — (Living well)
Includes index.
Summary: Describes how to prevent, prepare for, and respond calmly to various kinds of
emergency situations, including accidents, severe weather, and acts of violence.
  ISBN 1-59296-087-1 (Library Bound : alk. paper)
  1. Accidents—Juvenile literature. 2. Medical emergencies—Juvenile literature. [1.
Accidents. 2. Medical emergencies. 3. Safety.] I. Title. II. Series: Living well (Child's World
(Firm)
  HV675.5.R315 2004
  613.6'9—dc21   2003006285

TABLE OF CONTENTS

CHAPTER ONE

KEEPING COOL

Andrew and his sister Becky were watching TV while their mom was in the basement doing laundry. Suddenly they heard a thump and a crash. Andrew turned down the volume on the TV and listened.

"Mom?" he called.

There was no answer. Andrew got up and went to the basement door. "Mom?" he called again.

Slowly, he opened the door, and he couldn't believe what he saw. His mother was lying at the bottom of the stairs, and laundry was everywhere. She had fallen while coming up the steps! Andrew hurried down the stairs to his mother. She was **unconscious.** He touched her wrist and felt a pulse. He wanted to pick her up and take her to the couch, but he knew he shouldn't move her.

Andrew quickly went back upstairs and grabbed the phone. He dialed 9-1-1 and waited for an operator to answer. Calmly, Andrew told her his name and address, and he explained how his mother had fallen. The operator assured Andrew that an ambulance was on the way. He listened to her directions until she told him that he could hang up. Andrew's sister waited outside for the ambulance while he stayed with their mother. The ambulance arrived within minutes, and Becky led the **emergency** medical technicians (EMTs) inside. An EMT checked their mom, and then they moved her into the ambulance.

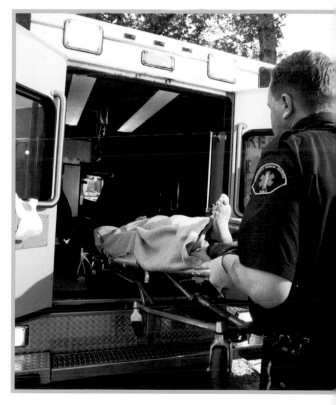

Emergency medical technicians put Andrew and Becky's mom into an ambulance.

"Hop in," one of the EMTs said to Andrew and Becky. "You can come with her to the hospital. She's gonna be fine. You guys did great."

Most days may seem very ordinary to you. Nothing seems **dangerous** about sitting at home and watching TV. But you never know when an emergency might occur. You can learn what to do if something does go wrong. The more you know, the safer you will be. Then, if you are faced with an emergency, you can trust what you have learned, and you'll know what to do.

Andrew and Becky rode in the ambulance with their mom and the EMTs.

CHAPTER TWO

WHAT KINDS OF
EMERGENCIES ARE THERE?

Emergencies can happen in your home. A family member might choke on a piece of food. Your sister might fall in the bathtub. A fire might start in your kitchen. Or a stranger might try to enter your house.

Emergencies can happen at school, too. A friend could get hurt on the playground. Another student could bring a **weapon** into your classroom.

In fact, emergencies can happen almost anywhere.

A stranger trying to enter your home is an emergency.

Your neighborhood might be affected by an emergency such as a tornado.

They can happen in your neighborhood as well. A **tornado** could hit your town. Or two cars could be in an **accident** on your corner.

All of these events may sound frightening to you. They are frightening because they affect you and people you care about. But you can help. You can learn how to prevent and prepare for emergencies. And, most important, you can learn what to do in an emergency. By planning ahead, you can help keep yourself and others safe.

The Red Cross

Throughout the world, the Red Cross is ready to help in emergencies. More than 170 countries have Red Cross offices. This group helps people who have experienced terrible events such as **hurricanes,** tornadoes, floods, or acts of violence. The Red Cross also organizes blood drives.

The organization's name comes from its flag: a red cross on a white background. The Red Cross was founded in Switzerland in 1863. Clara Barton helped start the American Red Cross in 1881.

The Red Cross often needs volunteers for its work. Talk to an adult if you'd like to learn more about the Red Cross. Someone from a local Red Cross office group could give a talk at your school, or you could visit their offices.

CHAPTER THREE

HOW CAN YOU PREVENT EMERGENCIES?

It is impossible to prevent every emergency. Emergencies will

sometimes occur, no matter how hard we try to

be safe. But it is still important to follow

certain safety rules and prevent as

many problems as we can.

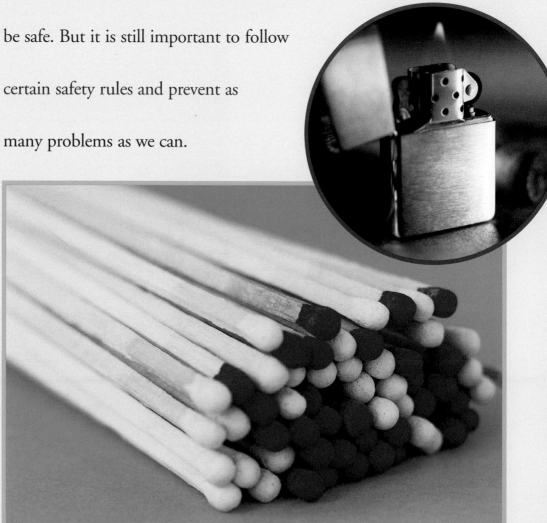

Playing with matches and lighters can cause fires.

In your home, there are lots of ways to stay safe. Never play with matches or lighters. Be sure to tell an adult if these items are left out. Matches and lighters can cause fires. And even little fires can become big fires very quickly.

Some people keep guns in their homes. If you ever find a gun, do not touch it. Tell an adult right away. A gun is not a toy, and you should never play with it. Adults should be sure that all guns are always kept locked up and unloaded.

Try not to leave toys or other items on steps or at the bottom of stairways. You or a member of your family could trip on them and fall. Never run up or down stairs. Always use the handrail.

If you see a gun that has been left out, do not touch it.
Instead, be sure to tell an adult immediately.

Many accidents in the home occur in the bathroom or in the kitchen. You should be extra careful in these rooms. Stay away from hot ovens and stoves. Wipe up spills on the floor so no one will slip and fall. Be sure not to use electric items around water. If they fall in the water, you could get shocked (electrocuted). You need to be careful of cleaning supplies, medicine and other poisons in kitchens and bathrooms. These items are very dangerous and can make you sick. Never eat or drink anything that you are unsure of. Some brightly colored bottles might contain cleaners or poisons. Do not handle them unless you have asked an adult if they are safe.

It's not safe to run on the stairs in your home. Someone might slip and fall.

Let your teacher know right away if you see a student at your school with a gun.

You can also prevent some emergencies by acting safely at school. Be careful of others on the playground and in the classrooms. Never push or shove other students. Always walk in the hallways—never run! If you see anyone with a gun or any kind of weapon, tell an adult right away. Some students may be very angry or sad. They may want to hurt others. Talk to your parents or a teacher if you ever hear a student say he wants to hurt someone.

CHAPTER FOUR

HOW CAN YOU
PREPARE FOR EMERGENCIES?

Sometimes you cannot prevent emergencies from happening. But there are many ways you can be ready for an emergency. You should make an emergency plan. Your school marks emergency exits and holds practice fire drills in case there is a fire at your school. Pay attention to the instructions from your teachers. You should also prepare for emergencies at home.

At home, you and your family should talk about a family emergency plan. This would include planning **escape routes** from your home and a family meeting place outside your home. When planning escape routes there should be two escape routes from every each room, in case one route is blocked you have another way out. There should be a family meeting place close to your home, so if you have to exit your home because of an

emergency, you know where to meet your family. This could

be at a neighbor's house or at a mailbox across the street. You

should practice your emergency plan, so everyone in your family

is prepared. Your house should have **smoke**

alarms on each level of your home.

It is a good idea to place them near

bedrooms, so you can hear them

Having smoke alarms and flashlights in your home will help you prepare for emergencies.

in your sleep. Remind your parents to test the smoke alarms monthly and change the batteries twice a year. It is also important to have flashlights around the house. Flashlights will help you find your way around the house in case your home loses electricity. Flashlights are safer than using candles if your house's electricity is out.

Remember to always keep your windows and doors locked at home. Never open your door to someone you do not know. A stranger may try to trick you to get into your house. Talk to your parents about who strangers are and how you should act around them. At home and at school, be extra careful around strangers. Never get into a stranger's car, and never tell a stranger your name.

You and your family should also have a list of emergency phone numbers. These could include your parents' work numbers, the neighbors' numbers, and numbers for the police and fire

department. But the most important number to remember for an

emergency is 9-1-1. If you live in a part of the country that does

not have 9-1-1 service, learn your local emergency number.

When you dial 9-1-1 or your local emergency number, you are connected to an emergency operator. The emergency operator will send help immediately. Do not hang up until the operator hangs up. He or she may

Some parts of the country do not have 9-1-1 service, so it's important to know your local emergency number.

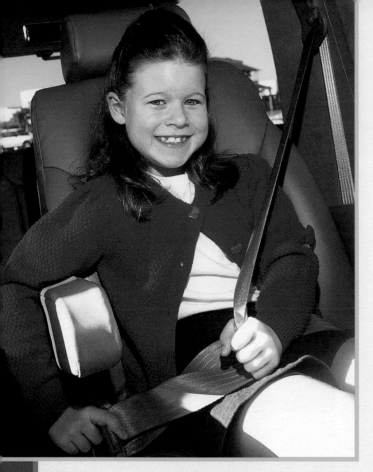

Be sure to buckle up when you ride in the car!

tell you what to do while waiting for help. Make sure your address is easily readable from the street. This will help police and other emergency workers find your home. If you do not have a readable address, ask your parents to fix the problem.

When riding in a car, always wear your seat belt. This will keep you safe if you are in an accident. Children should never sit near airbags. You are safest in the back seat.

As you get older, it is good to learn the basics about first aid. Knowing how to apply bandages and treat wounds may save someone's life. Also, talk to your parents about learning cardiopulmonary resuscitation, or CPR. CPR revives people who have stopped breathing. You could help someone whose heart has stopped beating. Another important skill to learn is the **Heimlich maneuver.** Knowing how to perform it could help someone who is choking.

Knowing about First Aid

First aid is the immediate help given to someone in an accident or other emergency. It can often save a person's life. One skill that you will learn in class is how to control bleeding. By applying a bandage to a wound and elevating the body part, you can help stop the bleeding. Another skill is performing cardiopulmonary resuscitation (CPR). CPR is the process of doing chest compressions and rescue breaths, to circulate blood with oxygen throughout the body. Remember that it is also important for you to not to get hurt, if you can't help the person without hurting yourself, call 9-1-1 or your local emergency number. You can learn more about first aid by contacting your local American Red Cross chapter or your school or local hospital might offer classes.

CHAPTER FIVE

WHAT DO YOU
DO IN AN EMERGENCY?

In most emergencies, the best advice is to call 9-1-1 or your local

emergency number. Calmly tell the operator your name and address,

and then explain what the problem is. Do not hang up the phone

until the operator tells you to. Depending on the type of emergency,

the operator may tell you what you need to do.

The best thing to do during an emergency is to call 9-1-1.
The operator will give you instructions and will send help.

For instance, if your mother is sick, the operator may tell you to wait with her until an ambulance gets there. But if someone has broken into your house, the operator may tell you to hide until the police arrive.

After you have called 9-1-1, do not make other calls. Keep the phone line open. If an ambulance is on the way, meet it outside or ask someone else to wait outside. If it is nighttime, use a flashlight or turn on an outdoor light to show the ambulance where you are.

If there is a fire at your home, do not call 9-1-1 at first. Instead, get out of the building as quickly as possible.

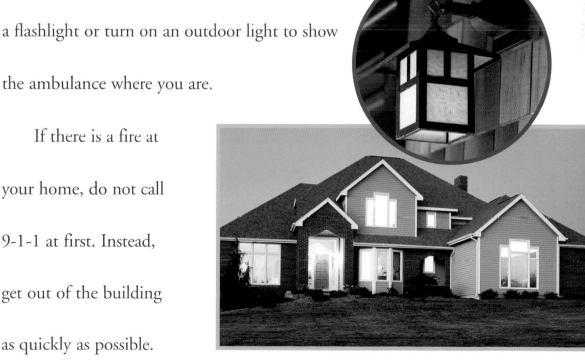

If an emergency happens at night, be sure to turn on outdoor lights. This will show the ambulance where to go.

Do not run, but exit quickly. Don't worry about toys or pets. The most important thing is to get out. Use the closest and safest exits you have planned with your family. If the fire exit is blocked by fire or smoke, use another way

If your room is filled with smoke, crawl low to the ground to safety.

out. Crawl on your hands and knees, so you stay below the smoke. If your clothing catches on fire, do not run. Instead, stop immediately and drop to the ground. Then roll on the ground until the flame is put out. Once you are safely outside and away from the fire, meet your family at the spot you decided on. Then someone can call 9-1-1 from a neighbor's home or from a cell phone.

If there is a fire at your school, follow the directions your teachers give you. Get out of the building as you have practiced in drills. Move quickly, but do not run. If there is smoke, crawl on your hands and knees. For other emergencies at school, listen to your teachers and follow their directions.

When the fire drill bell rings, calmly line up and follow your teacher out of the school.

For other kinds of emergencies at home, try to get to a safe place.

For instance, if there is a tornado or hurricane, you and your family

should move to the basement or a room on the first floor of your

home where there are no windows. These are the safest places to wait

out the storm. You should also cover your head and neck with your

hands to protect it from

falling objects.

If you are in a car

accident, do not try to get

out of the car unless it is

not safe to be in the car. If

you are hurt, you may cause

further injury by getting

out of the car. If anyone in

If you are in a car accident,
try to stay in the car unless it is unsafe to do so.

If you call 9-1-1 as a joke, you might prevent the operator from talking to someone else who actually needs help.

the car has a cell phone, use it to call

9-1-1 or try to get someone from outside

the car to call 9-1-1 for you.

Never call 9-1-1 unless you have an emergency. Don't call as

a joke or just to see what happens. Emergency operators are busy

helping people and saving lives. If you call for fun, you may be

keeping them from doing these important jobs.

CHAPTER SIX

WHAT IF YOU HAVE HAD
AN EMERGENCY?

f you have survived a fire or another emergency, you are probably

happy to be okay. But you may also be scared. You may be afraid to go

back to school if there was a fire there. Or you may be afraid of the car

if you were in an accident. You might have bad dreams about what

Being in an emergency is often scary, but talking to an adult might help you feel better.

happened. Just watching a certain show on TV might remind you of how scared you were. Even adults sometimes find it hard to deal with their feelings after being in an emergency. Such fears are normal, and you should not be ashamed to talk about them.

Tell a parent or teacher if you are having trouble. Adults can help you find ways to feel better about things again. Just talking to an adult or to a friend sometimes helps instead of keeping your feelings bottled up inside you. You also might want to draw or write about what happened. Some people who have been through an emergency like to talk to a therapist. A therapist is a doctor who treats your thoughts and feelings instead of your body. Talking to a therapist can help you understand why you are scared and how you can feel better. Getting back to normal may take a while. But your friends and family will be eager to help.

Glossary

accident (AK-sih-duhnt) An accident is an event that takes place unexpectedly and often involves people being hurt.

dangerous (DAYN-jur-uhss) Something that is dangerous is likely to cause harm. It is not safe.

emergency (i-MUR-juhn-see) An emergency is a sudden and dangerous situation. It requires immediate attention.

escape routes (ess-KAPE ROOTS) Escape routes are planned ways to leave a building in case of an emergency.

Heimlich maneuver (HIME-lik muh-NOO-ver) The Heimlich maneuver is an emergency action that helps dislodge food from a person's windpipe when he or she is choking.

hurricanes (HUR-uh-kanes) Hurricanes are strong storms with high winds.

smoke alarms (SMOHK uh-LARMZ) Smoke alarms, also called smoke detectors, warn you about smoke or fire by giving off a loud beep.

tornado (tor-NAY-doh) A tornado is a strong, dangerous column of air shaped like a funnel. It travels quickly and can destroy everything it touches.

unconscious (uhn-KON-shuhss) An unconscious person is alive but is not alert and cannot wake up.

weapon (WEP-uhn) A weapon is an item that can be used to hurt someone in a fight or an attack.

Questions and Answers about Emergencies

If someone at the front door says she is a police officer, is it okay to let her in? Maybe. First tell an adult. If you are home alone, talk to her through the door. A police officer will probably not ask to come in.

My best friend is joking around about bringing a gun to school and "taking care" of the playground bully. He's just kidding, right? He might not be. Talk to a teacher or parent about what your friend has said. If he is serious, someone could get hurt.

My dad just finished mowing the lawn and now says he has chest pains. What should I do? Call 9-1-1 right away. Then listen to and follow the instructions from the emergency operator.

The emergency operator for 9-1-1 is a stranger. Can I still tell him my name and address? The 9-1-1 operator is someone you can trust. You should give him whatever information he needs to help you.

Helping a Friend Learn about Emergencies

▶ You and your friend can pretend to make calls to 9-1-1 on a toy telephone. First, you make the call. Say your name and address, and then explain what the emergency is. Your friend can be the operator. Listen to the operator's instructions before hanging up. Then let your friend make the call while you play the operator.

▶ Help your friend learn about strangers. Talk about the adults you trust. Then talk about what to do if a stranger approaches you. Ask a parent or teacher to explain about strangers—such as firefighters and police officers—who are safe.

▶ Spend time with your friend learning about fire safety. Plan escape routes from both of your homes. Check both homes for smoke detectors. Encourage both families to have fire drills.

Did You Know?

▶ You should call 9-1-1 for emergencies involving fire or medical problems or any emergencies that require police assistance.

▶ The 9-1-1 emergency system was first created in 1968. Today, 9-1-1 works for nearly every home in the United States.

▶ You don't need money to call 9-1-1. Even from a pay phone, 9-1-1 calls are free.

▶ Quick-thinking kids can save lives by calling 9-1-1. It is the best way to get help in an emergency.

How to Learn More about Emergencies

At the Library: Nonfiction
Chaiet, Donna, and Francine Russell. *The Safe Zone.* New York: Morrow, 1998.

Gutman, Bill. *Harmful to Your Health.* Brookfield, Conn.: Twenty-First Century Books, 1997.

Levete, Sarah. *Looking after Myself.* Brookfield, Conn.: Millbrook Press, 1998.

Sanders, Pete, and Steve Myers. *Personal Safety.* Brookfield, Conn.: Copper Beech Books, 1999.

Schwartz, Linda. *What Would You Do? A Kid's Guide to Tricky and Sticky Situations.* Santa Barbara, Calif.: Learning Works, 1990.

Silverstein, Alvin, Virginia Silverstein, and Laura Silverstein Nunn. *Staying Safe.* Danbury, Conn.: Franklin Watts, 2000.

At the Library: Fiction
Beatty, Monica Driscoll, and Christie Allan-Piper. *Fire Night!* Santa Fe, N.M.: Health Press, 1998.

Byars, Betsy Cromer. *Tornado.* New York: HarperCollins, 1996.

On the Web
Visit our home page for lots of links about safety during emergencies: *http://www.childsworld.com/links.html*

Note to Parents, Teachers, and Librarians: We routinely verify our Web links to make sure they're safe, active sites—so encourage your readers to check them out!

Through the Mail or by Phone

American Red Cross National Headquarters
431 18th Street, N.W.
Washington, DC 20006
202/303-4498

National Center for Injury Prevention and Control
4770 Buford Highway, N.E.
Atlanta, GA 30341
770/488-1506

National SAFE KIDS Campaign
1301 Pennsylvania Avenue, N.W.
Suite 100
Washington, DC 20004
202/662-0600

National Capital Poison Control Center
3201 New Mexico Avenue, N.W.
Suite 310
Washington, DC 20016

Administrative Line:
202/362-3867
Emergency Hotline:
800/222-1222

The Nemours Center for Children's Health Media
Alfred I. duPont Hospital for Children
1600 Rockland Road
Wilmington, DE 19803
302/651-4046

U.S. Consumer Product Safety Commission
Washington, DC 20207
800/638-2772

Index

About the Author

Lucia Raatma received her bachelor's degree in English literature from the University of South Carolina and her master's degree in cinema studies from New York University. She has written a wide range of books for young people. When she is not researching or writing, she enjoys going to movies, practicing yoga, and spending time with her husband, their daughter, and their golden retriever. She lives in New York.